Dear Francine,

Hope you enjoy this little book.

Wishing you a very sweet and prosperous New Year. Hope to see you soon

Happy Holidays!

Love,

Randy

The Frookie Cookie Cookbook

THE

Frookie Cookie Cookbook

Randye Worth, M.A., R.D.
Registered Dietitian

William Morrow and Company, Inc.
New York

It is the policy of William Morrow and Company, Inc., and its imprints and affiliates, recognizing the importance of preserving what has been written, to print the books we publish on acid-free paper, and we exert our best efforts to that end.

Library of Congress Cataloging-in-Publication Data

Worth, Randye.
    The Frookie cookie cookbook / Randye Worth.
        p.   cm.
    Includes index.
    ISBN 0-688-11911-5
    1. Cookies.   2. Fruit juices.   I. R.W. Frookies, Inc.
    II. Title.
    TX772.W67   1994
    641.8'654—dc20   94-18569
                                                          CIP

Printed in the United States of America

First Edition

1 2 3 4 5 6 7 8 9 10

BOOK DESIGN BY RICHARD ORIOLO

Acknowledgments

Beverly Malkin Rappaport

My devoted mother, retired dietitian, gourmet cook, and best friend, whose recipe contributions and baking expertise are evident throughout this book. She was instrumental in helping me develop the original recipes for R. W. Frookie cookies. Once again, I have called on her for help. Much love and thanks!

Edward Rappaport

My loyal father, taste tester and fan, for his encouragement and support.

Richard Scott Worth

My loving, talented husband, entrepreneur and co-creator of R. W. Frookie Cookies and "Good For You Foods," for his undying enthusiasm, energy, support, and encouragement. Much love and thanks!

Helen Malkin Pinkert

My dear Aunt Helen, for her everlasting love and concern and for her mandelbrot recipe.

Megan Newman

My inspirational editor, whose insight and talent gave focus to this book.

Susan Sinnenburg, Mary Katherine Bishop, and Jaime Castantine

My enthusiastic assistants, for their patience and diligence in typing and organizing the manuscript.

Bill Adler

Whose marketing savvy and vision brought us all together and ultimately made this book possible.

Contents

Bar Cookies

Drop Cookies

Refrigerator Cookies

No-Bake Cookies

Savory Cookies

Icings and Spreads

The Frookie Cookie Cookbook

Introduction

Ever since I can remember, cooking has been a major part of my life. I was inspired at a young age by my mother, a gourmet cook and dietitian. I have vivid memories of helping her prepare cookies, especially rugelach. Making them was practically an all-day affair. It seemed to me that my mother made them by instinct, since she never used a recipe.

She, too, learned most of her cookie recipes from watching her mother. I was her willing co-chef, bringing ingredients from the cupboard and eagerly watching as she mixed the dough. She rewarded my efforts by letting me lick the bowl and the mixer blades. When the delicious rugelach were done, the sweet smell of cinnamon, sugar, and butter wafted through the house. Then my mother would dole them out one by one, as if they were precious gems. Her message was loud and clear: Cookies were a once-in-a-while treat and a reward for good behavior.

After earning a degree in dietetics from Syracuse University and a master's degree in food and nutrition from New York University, I became a nutritionist and, eventually, cookbook author. My career took a romantic turn in 1982, when I met my husband-to-be, Richard, at the New York Gourmet Food Show. At that point Richard was an industry pioneer as the founder of Sorrell Ridge, one of the first companies to make fruit juice–sweetened jams and jellies. I was talking to his food broker when Richard frantically interrupted our conversation. "I have to leave my booth!" he exclaimed. I responded, "Where do you think you're going?" He replied, "That sounds like a heavy offer!" "Well, it is." Little did I know that I would marry this man and together we would create R. W. Frookies, The Good for You Cookie company.

A few years later, Richard had sold Sorrell Ridge and was itching to do something new. We were pleased with the already successful fruit juice–sweetened concept and wanted to develop a new product that was fun to eat yet good for you. Richard focused on cookies and thought of the name Frookie: fruit + cookie = Frookie. I started developing Frookies in my tiny Manhattan apartment kitchen. After three years of hard work, we launched Frookies in 1988. Today, over thirty varieties of R. W. Frookie cookies are sold in major supermarket chains, independent groceries, and natural food stores across the country.

Our goal at Frookies is to make the perfect cookie, one with great taste and the right ingredients: low in saturated fat, fruit juice–sweetened, and all natural.

The Frookie Cookie Cookbook was created so you could make healthy Frookies at home. This book is truly a labor of love: While I was developing the recipes, I was pregnant with my first son, Benjamin. Following an all-natural, low-fat, low-sugar diet, I happily indulged in a daily sampling of homemade Frookie Cookies. The cookies in this book satisfied my craving for sweets and provided delicious chemical-free treats.

Nothing compares to the taste of "real" food. As a nutritionist, I don't believe that foods laden with artificial ingredients are nutritionally superior to natural foods, even though in some cases these "fake" or imitation foods may be lower in calories. In fact, most nutritionists today would argue that butter in moderate amounts is a better choice than artificially processed margarine. I would rather have less of a natural ingredient than more of an artificial one, in terms of both good nutrition and taste appeal. The key word is *moderation.*

With these recipes, I'll show you how to achieve equally good if not better results using fruit juice or pure fructose (fruit sugar)—key ingredients in all Frookies' products—rather than sugar. The recipes in this book are designed to please everyone—even people on diabetic diets. Therefore, I have included caloric, carbohydrate, fat, and diabetic exchange information. There are breakfast cookies, lunch-box cookies, bar cookies, drop cookies, after-school cookies, gift cookies, special-occasion cookies, and even savory cookies. And, of course, many adaptations of my mother's recipes appear in the book.

The advantages of making your own cookies? Freshness, satisfaction, homemade quality, originality, and, most important, the sharing of delicious gifts with family and friends. I hope this book will inspire you to create your own magnificent cookies. Remember, . . . A Frookie a Day Keeps the Blues Away. Happy baking!

A Word About Sweeteners

Most baked goods and desserts are made with some form of sucrose, such as granulated sugar, corn syrup, or brown sugar (white sugar with molasses added). Sucrose in these forms is highly refined and depleted of any nutrients. Sucrose sweeteners not only add empty calories, but actually deplete the body of valuable nutrients without adding any that are required to metabolize the sugar. In addition, they trigger an overproduction of insulin, which in turn stimulates fat production and weight gain.

Poor nutrition and high sugar intake can eventually lead to diabetes. For these reasons, doctors and nutritionists strongly recommend that people avoid eating too much sugar.

The Frookie Cookie Cookbook will teach you how to satisfy your sweet tooth without sucrose. All of the sweeteners described below contain some vitamins and minerals and are easily metabolized by your body without depleting its supply of nutrients.

FRUIT JUICE CONCENTRATES contain vitamins and minerals and are naturally sweet. They are found in the frozen food section of supermarkets and are available in a variety of flavors. Be sure you buy *unsweetened* fruit juice concentrate, without added sugar. I find that apple juice concentrate, readily found in stores, works well in baking. White grape juice works even better due to its milder flavor, but is sometimes hard to find in unsweetened concentrated form. You can also try mixing a variety of fruit juice concentrates together—or use several different kinds of fruit juices with other natural sweeteners such as dried fruit, fruit juice—sweetened preserves, or fructose. When substituting fruit juice concentrates for sugar in a recipe, reduce the amount of liquid in the dough by the amount of fruit juice being added. For drop, rolled, or refrigerator cookies, fruit juice concentrates work best when used with fructose or fruit juice–sweetened preserves.

CRYSTALLINE FRUCTOSE (fruit sugar) is identical to the fructose naturally present in fruits, berries, and vegetables. It is a white crystalline powder that looks and tastes like sugar, and it is sold under the brand name of Estee. Fructose can be found in the diet or sugar sections of the supermarket or in natural food stores.

Crystalline fructose should not be confused with conventional corn syrups or high-fructose corn syrups, which are only partly fructose, the rest being sucrose and water. High-fructose corn syrup is metabolized in the same manner as sucrose.

Crystalline fructose is metabolized much more slowly than sucrose, or table sugar, meaning that the body releases less insulin. Fructose, therefore does not cause the extreme highs and lows in blood sugar that sucrose does. As a result, it is gentle on the body's metabolic system and in most cases can be tolerated by people with diabetes. *It is important, however, that people with diabetes check with their doctor or nutritionist before consuming fructose.*

Crystalline fructose is a wonderful sweetener for baked goods and can be substituted for sugar on an equal basis in most cases. Cookies with fructose tend to brown more quickly than those made with granulated sugar, so it is best to lower the oven temperatures specified in conventional recipes by 25 degrees. For example, if the oven temperature for a sugar-based cookie recipe is 375°F, the fructose- or fruit juice–based cookies should be baked at 350°F.

Fructose tends to hold moisture in baked goods. If cookies soften over time (especially in humid climates), place in a 300°F oven for five to ten minutes to crisp.

If you cannot find fructose in your store, write or call:

The Estee Corporation
169 Lackawanna Ave.
Parsippany, NJ 07054
1–800–34–ESTEE

The Fourteen Secrets of Great Cookie Baking

1. Preheat the oven at least 15 minutes before baking.

2. Measuring Dry Ingredients
- Spoon ingredients into a dry-measure measuring cup and level off the excess by passing a straight edge evenly across the rim of the cup.
- Do not sift flour before measuring it unless the recipe specifies sifting.
- Do not tap the measuring cup or pack the flour into the cup before leveling it off.

3. Mixing Doughs
- To cream butter means to beat it until it is fluffy and lemon-colored.
- When creaming butter with fructose, beat until the fructose is incorporated into the butter, and the mixture is light and fluffy.
- Do not overwork the dough once the flour is added to the butter mixture: Overmixing toughens the dough.

4. Shaping Doughs
- The dough for rolled and molded cookies should be chilled for at least one hour prior to baking to prevent the cookies from spreading while baking.
- Shape or roll doughs to an even thickness to ensure even baking.
- Flour the work surface and the rolling pin well to keep the dough from sticking.
- Always brush off the excess flour from the dough before transferring cookies to baking sheets.
- Do not roll the dough too thin or it will be difficult to transfer the cut-out shapes to the cookie sheets.
- Gather scraps of dough into a ball, chill, and re-roll.

5. Use cookie sheets or jelly-roll pans.
- Dark cookie sheets absorb heat more readily than light ones and, as a result, cookies baked on them may brown too much on the bottom.
- Cookies baked in pans with sides 2 inches or higher do not bake evenly.
- Teflon-coated pans or cookie sheets do not need to be greased.
- Lightly grease regular cookie sheets with unsalted butter or spray with no-stick cooking spray.
- For delicate cookies, line the pan with parchment paper or aluminum foil so that the cookies can be peeled off easily when slightly cooled.
- Baking sheets should always be cool before cookies are placed on it so they will not melt and lose their shape.
- Always fill the sheet to ensure even baking.
- In general, place cookies about one inch apart on the baking sheet.

6. Placement of pans in the oven
- If using only one large baking sheet or two small ones, use the middle oven rack and be sure the pan or pans are at least two inches away from the oven walls.

- When using two smaller pans, make sure they are placed an even distance from each other and the oven walls.

7. To bake in quantity, use two racks in the oven.
- Prepare one pan of cookies and place it on the lower rack of the oven. While it bakes, prepare another pan of cookies. Then transfer the first pan to the upper rack to finish baking and put the second pan on the lower rack. After baking about five minutes, gently rotate the racks from back to front so the cookies bake evenly.

8. Use a timer.
- Proper timing will prevent cookies from burning.

9. Testing
- In general, cookies are done when they have a golden hue and the edges are lightly browned.
- Bar cookies are done when a cake tester or toothpick inserted in the center comes out clean.
- Frookies tend to burn easily, so it is wise to check them a few minutes before they are due to come out of the oven. Check them quickly so the oven does not lose heat.

10. Cool cookies on wire racks.
- Remove cookies from the baking sheet after cooling a minute or two on the pan for easier removal, or they will continue to bake.

11. Store cookies properly.
- Most cookies should be stored at room temperature.
- Crisp cookies should be kept in a container with a loose cover; soft ones should be kept airtight.
- To keep cookies moist, place a fresh apple wedge or piece of bread in the cookie container.
- Never store crisp cookies with soft ones—they will become soggy.
- Cookies with fructose or fruit juice tend to absorb moisture from the air.

- If cookies become limp, place them on an ungreased baking sheet and crisp in a 300°F oven for five minutes.

12. Take advantage of your refrigerator and freezer when making cookies.
- Roll cookie dough in wax paper or aluminum foil to prevent drying and then store in the refrigerator for up to one week or for even longer in the freezer.
- Thaw most frozen doughs before proceeding with the recipe. However, frozen bar doughs that have been frozen in the baking pan do not have to thaw before baking: Just increase the baking time by ten minutes.
- Let baked cookies cool completely before freezing them. Wrap them in wax paper or foil and store in airtight plastic containers. Thaw them in the containers to prevent them from becoming soggy, and crisp them for five to ten minutes in a 300°F oven.

13. Giving Cookies
- Freeze a dozen cookies each time you bake, and you will soon have an assorted collection for giving.
- All the cookies in this book are good travelers, provided they are packaged well: Wrap each cookie individually in clear cellophane, wax paper, or aluminum foil. Layer them between wax paper in a tin with a tight-fitting lid. If mixing cookies, layer heavier ones beneath fragile ones. Fill empty spaces with popcorn or tissue paper.
- Be sure to decorate the tin with some pretty ribbon for the perfect gift!

14. Mailing Cookies
- Select a cardboard box that is only slightly larger than the cookie tin to minimize shifting.
- Layer the bottom of the box with crumpled paper or bubble wrap.
- Pack more paper on top of and around the tin.
- Fasten the box securely and label the package "Fragile and Perishable."

The Frookie Cookie Cookbook

Cookie Equipment

You need not invest in fancy equipment to bake cookies, but you do need some basic tools in addition to measuring cups, spoons, and a spatula.

1. *Cookie Sheets*   Cookie sheets should be made of heavyweight aluminum. If you have only lightweight cookie sheets, double them up to prevent burning. Remember that dark sheets absorb more heat and often result in burned cookie bottoms. Shiny heavy-gauge aluminum sheets with only one or two rims allow for air circulation and are best for baking cookies.

2. *Jelly-Roll Pans*   These are baking pans with a low rim all around. They are used for baking cookie batters that need sides to contain them—such as bar cookies. The usual size is $15\frac{1}{2} \times 10\frac{1}{2} \times 1$ inch.

3. *Cooling Racks*   These are raised wire mesh grids that allow air to circulate around cookies as they cool. Cooling on wire racks guards against soggy cookies.

4. *Double Boilers* These are ideal for melting chocolate so it does not scorch or burn. You can improvise by placing a saucepan or heatproof bowl into or over a larger pan, deep enough so that the boiling water does not come in contact with the upper pan or bowl.

5. *Sifters* These are readily available in supermarkets and cookware stores. If you do not have a sifter, you can use a strainer: Place the flour or other dry ingredient, such as cocoa, in the strainer and gently tap to sift it through.

6. *Grater or Zester* These are handy for quickly grating citrus zest. A zester is a small tool designed to cut only the colored portion of the peel from citrus fruits. You can, however, use a vegetable peeler to pare thin strips of zest, taking care to avoid the bitter white pith. Then mince the zest as fine as possible with a sharp knife.

7. *Rolling Pins* Available in metal or wood, these are essential for making rolled cookies. I prefer to use a wooden rolling pin because it does not absorb heat. Therefore, the dough is less likely to stick to the rolling pin, making it easier to handle.

8. *Cookie Cutters* Cookie cutters are available in every shape imaginable and are especially fun to use when baking with children. If you do not have cookie cutters, use an inverted glass to cut out rounds.

9. *Electric Mixers* These are ideal for creaming butter, making meringues, and mixing heavy or sticky doughs. Stand electric mixers come with their own bowls that fit on a platform underneath the mixer blades so you do not have to hold them. Hand-held mixers are less expensive and can be placed into almost any deep bowl. They do require a bit more work, however, because they must be held by hand.

10. *Food Processors* A food processor (I prefer Cuisinart, for its strength and durability) works best for grinding nuts and chopping raisins and dried fruit. Take care not to overprocess, or you will end up with a nut butter or fruit pastes. Some people prefer to use food processors for making cookie doughs and batters; however, I find the machine tends to overwork and toughen the dough. I recommend using an electric mixer.

11. *Nut Grinder* If you do not have a food processor, you can pulverize nuts in a rotary grater.

12. *Rubber Scraper* These are handy for scraping batter from the sides of the mixer bowl.

13. *Wooden Spoons* Wooden spoons are perfect for mixing raisins, nuts, and other such ingredients into doughs and batters.

14. *Pastry Bag* Pastry bags are versatile decorating tools, with many tips to choose from, for piping icings and frostings.

Ingredients

Butter: I always use unsalted (sweet) butter in cookie doughs because it imparts a wonderful flavor to baked goods. Do not use whipped butter—it has air pumped into it and cannot be substituted for stick butter.

Butter that is to be creamed should be room temperature. To bring butter to room temperature quickly, cut into small pieces. Never attempt to warm butter in the oven or microwave: It will melt.

Butter keeps at least two weeks in the refrigerator and can be stored almost indefinitely in the freezer.

Chocolate: The only chocolates used in this book contain no sugar.

- Unsweetened Chocolate
  Unsweetened chocolate is available packaged in one-ounce squares. I prefer the rich "European" flavor of Baker's chocolate.
  Melt chocolate in a microwave-safe bowl in the microwave or in the top of a double boiler set over very hot, not boiling, water.

- Cocoa

  Be sure to buy unsweetened cocoa powder. I prefer to use a Dutch-process cocoa such as Droste, Van Houten, or Lindt because the flavor is rich and less bitter than nonalkalized cocoa. In a pinch, however, I find the best alternative is Hershey's nonalkalized cocoa. (Never use instant cocoa or hot chocolate mixes.)

Eggs: Large eggs were used in testing these recipes.

When making meringues, always start with room-temperature egg whites. Be sure that no fat, such as a drop of egg yolk, comes in contact with egg whites, as this will inhibit foam production and keep the egg whites from becoming stiff. If a drop of yolk or fat does spill into egg whites, use a piece of shell to remove it. Cream of tartar may be added during the beating process to keep the egg whites stiff.

Flour: The recipes in this book use either unbleached all-purpose flour or whole wheat flour. You may substitute whole wheat flour for half of the unbleached all-purpose flour in most recipes, but the cookies will be heavier in texture. In most cases, I do not recommend substituting whole wheat flour for all of the all-purpose flour because the cookies will be very dense.

Fruit Juice-Sweetened Jams and Preserves:
Made with fruit, concentrated fruit juice, and pectin, these products have only about fourteen calories per teaspoon. They work exceptionally well as sweeteners in baking, but you cannot substitute them directly for sugar. They work best in combination with other sweeteners. They can be substituted in any recipe calling for sugar-sweetened preserves. I prefer Sorrell Ridge Fruit Juice–Sweetened Preserves.

Molasses: Molasses is made from sugarcane juice; however, it contains significant amounts of calcium, potassium, iron, and other vitamins and minerals. The flavor is too strong to use as the sole sweetener in cookies, so it is usually used with other sweeteners. It is an excellent substitute for brown sugar when used together with fructose.

Nuts: In recipes calling for nuts, you can use any variety of *unsalted* nuts.

To blanch whole almonds, cover them with boiling water and set aside for ten minutes. Drain, cover the nuts with cold water, and let sit several minutes longer. The skins should peel off easily.

Store nuts in the refrigerator or freezer in airtight containers. They do become rancid over time, so be sure to taste them before adding to a recipe.

Vegetable Oil: Most vegetable oils (with the exception of palm and coconut) are low in saturated fats and contain no cholesterol. For baking, choose a light flavorless vegetable oil, such as corn, safflower, or soybean. Do not attempt to substitute oil for butter without making other adjustments in the recipe, or the dough will be oily and too soft.

Ingredient Equivalents

Apricots	1 pound	3 cups
Baking chocolate	8 ounces	8 squares
Butter	1 pound	2 cups
Coconut, shredded or flaked	4 ounces	1⅓ cups
Cream cheese	8 ounces	1 cup
	3 ounces	6 tablespoons
Dates, pitted and cut up	1 pound	2½ cups
Figs, dried, cut up	1 pound	2⅔ cups
Lemon juice	1 medium lemon	2 to 3 tablespoons
Lemon zest, grated	1 medium lemon	1½ to 3 teaspoons
Nuts, shelled		
almonds	1 pound	3½ cups
peanuts	1 pound	3 cups
pecans	1 pound	4 cups
walnuts	1 pound	5 cups
Orange zest, grated	1 medium orange	1 to 2 tablespoons
Prunes, dried, pitted	1 pound	2¼ cups
Raisins	1 pound	2¾ cups
Sour cream	8 ounces	1 scant cup

Bar Cookies

Bar cookies are easy because they do not have to be shaped. They are baked as a slab and then cut into bars or squares.

Chocolate and a strawberry cream cheese filling are a delicious combination in these cake-like bars. A Dutch-process European cocoa, such as Droste, Van Houten, or Lindt, gives a rich chocolate flavor. Serve with low-fat frozen yogurt for an extra-special treat.

Makes 36 Bars

Marbled Chocolate-Strawberry Cream Cheese Bars

Strawberry Cream Cheese Filling

One 8-ounce package cream cheese, softened
½ cup fruit juice–sweetened strawberry jam, such as Sorrell Ridge
1 large egg, beaten

1½ cups unbleached all-purpose flour
1 cup fructose
¼ cup Dutch-process cocoa
1 cup water
½ cup vegetable oil
1 tablespoon cider vinegar
1 teaspoon baking soda
1 teaspoon vanilla extract
½ teaspoon salt

Preheat the oven to 350°F. Lightly butter a 9-inch square baking pan or spray with no-stick cooking spray.

To make the filling, in a medium bowl, beat the cream cheese with a mixer until smooth and creamy. Beat in the jam, then beat in the egg until well blended. Set aside.

In a large bowl, combine all the remaining ingredients. Using an electric mixer, beat at low speed for 1 minute. Or combine in the bowl of a food processor fitted with the metal blade and pulse for 30 seconds, or until blended, scraping the sides of the bowl as necessary.

Spread half the batter evenly in the prepared baking pan. Using a spoon, spread the cream cheese filling on top. Spread the remaining batter evenly over the filling. Gently swirl a knife through the batter for a marbled effect.

Bake for about 30 minutes, or until a toothpick inserted in the center comes out clean. Cool in the pan on a wire rack. Cut into 2¼ × 1-inch bars.

Store: Up to 4 days covered and refrigerated.

Nutrition Information per Serving
(1 Bar)

Calories: 100

Carbohydrate: 14 grams

Fat: 5 grams

Exchanges:
1 Fruit + 1 Fat

Hawaiian Crunch Bars

Filling

4 cups chopped pitted dates

Two 8-ounce cans unsweetened crushed pineapple, undrained

¾ cup water

1 teaspoon vanilla extract

Crumb Crust Topping

1½ cups whole wheat flour

1½ cups old-fashioned rolled oats

½ teaspoon salt

¾ cup (1½ sticks) unsalted butter, softened

½ cup chopped walnuts

½ cup flaked unsweetened coconut

To make the filling, combine all the ingredients in a large nonreactive sauce-pan. Simmer uncovered, stirring occasionally, over low heat for 8 to 10 minutes, until slightly thickened. Let cool to room temperature.

Preheat the oven to 350°F. Lightly butter a 13 × 9-inch glass baking dish or metal pan or spray with no-stick cooking spray.

To make the crust/topping, combine all the ingredients in the bowl of a food processor fitted with the metal blade and pulse until well blended. Or combine the ingredients in a large bowl and using an electric mixer on medium speed, blend well. Pat half the crumbs firmly into the bottom and up the sides of the prepared pan. Spread the date mixture evenly over the crumbs. Top with the remaining crumbs. Pat down well, pressing down with fingertips. Bake for 40 to 45 minutes, or until light brown on top. Cool in the pan on a wire rack. Cut into 2 × 1¼-inch bars.

Variation: Substitute 2 cups chopped dried apricots for half the dates.

Store: Up to 2 days covered at room temperature or up to 5 days refrigerated.

Nutrition Information per Serving
(1 Bar)

Calories: 70

Carbohydrate: 13 grams

Fat: 2 grams

Exchanges:
1 Fruit + ½ Fat

This is a soothing winter dessert. Serve with a dollop of whipped cream and piping hot coffee or tea for a memorable finale to brunch or dinner.

Makes 50 Bars

Nutrition Information per Serving
(1 Bar)

Calories: 75

Carbohydrate: 12 grams

Fat: 3 grams

Exchanges:
1 Fruit + ¾ Fat

Raisin Spice Bars

1 cup raisins

1 cup frozen unsweetened apple juice concentrate, thawed

¼ cup water

½ cup (1 stick) unsalted butter, softened

2 cups unbleached all-purposed flour

1 teaspoon baking soda

½ teaspoon baking powder

½ teaspoon salt

½ teaspoon ground cloves

½ teaspoon ground cinnamon

1 large egg, beaten

1 cup chopped walnuts

Preheat the oven to 350°F. Lightly butter and flour a 10 × 15-inch jelly-roll pan or spray with no-stick cooking spray and dust with flour.

Combine the raisins, juice, and water in a medium saucepan and bring to a boil. Lower the heat, add the butter, and simmer for 5 minutes. Transfer to a large bowl and let cool completely.

Sift together the flour, baking soda, baking powder, salt, and spices into a medium bowl.

Stir the egg into the raisin mixture until well blended. Stir in the dry ingredients, and mix until smooth. Spread evenly in the prepared pan. Sprinkle the chopped nuts over the top.

Bake for 20 to 25 minutes, or until a toothpick inserted into the center comes out clean. Cool in the pan on a wire rack. Cut into 3 × 1-inch bars.

Store: Up to 3 days, covered, at room temperature.

The Frookie Cookie Cookbook

Apricot Raisin Bars

1 cup (2 sticks) plus 2 tablespoons butter, softened

1⅓ cups fructose

2 large eggs

1 teaspoon vanilla extract

2½ cups unbleached all-purpose flour

1 teaspoon baking powder

1 cup raisins

½ cup apricot fruit juice–sweetened jam, such as Sorrell Ridge

Preheat the oven to 350°F. Lightly butter a 13 × 9-inch baking pan or spray with no-stick cooking spray.

In a large bowl, using an electric mixer, beat the butter and fructose until creamy, about 1 minute. Beat in the eggs and vanilla until smooth. Stir in the flour and baking powder. Stir in the raisins. Spread the batter evenly in the prepared pan.

Melt the apricot jam in a small pan. Or microwave on high power for 1 minute. Spread the jam evenly over the batter. Bake for 13 to 15 minutes, or until light brown on the edges. Cool in the pan on a wire rack. Cut into bars about 2 × 1¼ inches.

Store: Up to 5 days covered at room temperature.

Your guests will savor these rich buttery bars, enhanced with the natural sweetness of apricots. Quick and easy, they are perfect for last-minute gatherings.

Makes 46 Bars

Nutrition Information per Serving
(1 Bar)

Calories: 90

Carbohydrate: 12 grams

Fat: 4 grams

Exchanges:
½ Bread + 1 Fat

The flavors of pumpkin and cream cheese marry in these bars for a delicious Thanksgiving treat. If you're not counting calories, serve with vanilla ice cream.

Makes 46 Bars

Pumpkin Cream Cheese Bars

½ cup (1 stick) unsalted butter, softened
1 cup fructose
2 large eggs
1 cup canned pumpkin puree (unsweetened)
1 tablespoon molasses
1 cup unbleached all-purpose flour
1 teaspoon baking powder
½ teaspoon baking soda
½ teaspoon salt
2 teaspoons ground cinnamon
1 teaspoon ground ginger
½ teaspoon ground cloves
1 cup dark raisins
½ cup chopped walnuts

Cream Cheese Filling

5 tablespoons unsalted butter, softened
Two 3-ounce packages cream cheese, softened
⅓ cup fructose
2 large eggs
1 teaspoon vanilla extract
2 tablespoons unbleached all-purpose flour

Browned Butter Frosting (recipe follows)

Preheat the oven to 350°F. Lightly butter a 13 × 9-inch baking pan or spray with no-stick cooking spray.

In a large bowl using an electric mixer, cream the butter and fructose at high speed for about 1 minute. Beat in the eggs one at a time, then beat in the pumpkin and molasses. Combine the flour, baking powder, baking soda, salt, cinnamon, ginger, and cloves. On medium speed, gradually add to the pumpkin batter, mixing well. Stir in the raisins and walnuts.

To make the filling, in a small bowl, using an electric mixer, cream the butter and cream cheese. Beat in fructose, then, individually, the eggs, vanilla, and flour. Beat on medium speed until well blended, scraping the sides of the bowl occasionally.

Spread half of the pumpkin batter evenly in the prepared pan. Spoon the cream cheese filling evenly over the batter. Spread the remaining pumpkin batter evenly over the filling. Swirl a knife through the batter for a marbled effect.

Bake for 35 to 40 minutes or until the top springs back when lightly touched. Cool in the pan on a wire rack.

Frost with Browned Butter Frosting. Cut into bars about 2 × 1¼ inches. (Refrigerate any leftover bars.)

Browned Butter Frosting

  3 tablespoons unsalted butter
  1 cup fructose
  2 tablespoons milk
  1 teaspoon vanilla extract

Melt the butter in a small saucepan over low heat. Stir in the fructose. Cook, stirring, until the fructose has dissolved and the mixture is light brown in color. Remove from the heat. Stir in the milk and vanilla and stir until smooth and of spreading consistency.

Store: Up to 5 days covered and refrigerated.

Nutrition Information per Serving
(1 Bar)

Calories: 130

Carbohydrate: 18 grams

Fat: 6 grams

Exchanges:
1 Bread + 1 Fat

Makes 1 Cup

These are a delicious after-school snack, packed with vitamins, fiber, and love. Wrap the squares individually in plastic wrap and include in your family's lunch boxes.

Makes 16 Squares

Orange Granola Coconut Squares

Crust

½ cup (1 stick) unsalted butter, softened
¼ cup fructose
½ cup whole wheat flour
¼ cup unbleached all-purpose flour
¼ cup wheat germ
¼ teaspoon salt

Granola Layer

1 tablespoon whole wheat flour
1 teaspoon baking powder
¼ teaspoon salt
2 large eggs
½ cup fruit juice–sweetened orange marmalade
½ cup granola
½ cup shredded unsweetened coconut

Preheat the oven to 350°F. Lightly butter a 9-inch square baking pan or spray with no-stick cooking spray.

To make the crust, in a medium bowl, using an electric mixer at high speed, cream the butter and fructose for 1 minute. Beat in the flours, wheat germ, and salt until a crumbly dough forms. Press the dough evenly into the prepared pan. Bake for about 20 minutes, until lightly browned.

While the crust is baking, combine the flour, baking powder, and salt in a small bowl. In a medium bowl, beat the eggs with an electric mixer until light and lemon-colored, about 1 minute. Beat in the orange marmalade. Stir in the dry ingredients, then stir in the granola and coconut. Pour the mixture over the partially baked crust.

Bake for 20 minutes, or until lightly browned on top. Cool in the pan on a wire rack. Cut into sixteen 2¼-inch squares.

Store: Up to 3 days covered at room temperature.

Nutrition Information per Serving
(1 square)

Calories: 100

Carbohydrate: 11 grams

Fat: 5 grams

Exchanges:
1 Fruit + 1 Fat

Here is a great way to sneak some veggies into your kids' diets. These delicious bars are luscious, moist, and full of flavor. If desired, frost with Cream Cheese Icing (page 91).

Makes 16 Squares

Nutrition Information per Serving
(1 Square)

Calories: 80

Carbohydrate: 12 grams

Fat: 3 grams

Exchanges:
1 Fruit + ½ Fat

Zucchini Applesauce Nut Squares

¼ cup corn, soybean, or safflower oil

⅓ cup fructose

1 large egg

1 cup unsweetened applesauce

1¼ cups whole wheat flour

½ teaspoon baking soda

½ teaspoon ground cinnamon

¼ teaspoon ground nutmeg

⅛ teaspoon salt

1 cup shredded zucchini, well drained

½ cup chopped walnuts

Preheat the oven to 350°F. Lightly butter a 9-inch square baking pan or spray with no-stick cooking spray.

In a large bowl, using an electric mixer at medium speed, beat the oil, fructose, egg, and applesauce for 1 minute. Mix flour, baking soda, spices, and salt and add gradually to the applesauce batter, mixing well. Stir in the zucchini and walnuts. Spread the batter evenly in the prepared pan.

Bake for 20 to 30 minutes, until lightly browned and a tester comes out clean when inserted in middle of pan. Cool in the pan on a wire rack. Cut into sixteen 2¼-inch squares.

Store: Up to 3 days covered and refrigerated.

Black Raspberry–Almond Squares

1 cup granola

¼ cup wheat germ

2 tablespoons unsalted butter, melted

2 large eggs, beaten

1 cup unblanched almonds, chopped

½ cup fruit juice–sweetened black raspberry preserves, such as Sorrell Ridge

1 teaspoon vanilla extract

Preheat the oven to 325°F. Line an 8-inch square baking pan with parchment paper, or lightly butter or spray with no-stick cooking spray.

Combine the granola, wheat germ, and melted butter in a small bowl, and mix well. Press 1 cup of this crumb mixture evenly into the prepared pan.

In a medium bowl, combine the eggs, almonds, preserves, and vanilla and mix well. Spoon over the crumb crust. Sprinkle the remaining crumbs over the top.

Bake for 20 to 25 minutes until lightly browned. Cool slightly in the pan on a wire rack. Cut into 25 squares.

Store: Up to 3 days covered at room temperature.

Delicious, fruity, and crunchy, these squares taste like a berry cobbler when served warm. You can dress them up with whipped cream for special occasions or serve on their own for a satisfying snack.

Makes 25 Squares

Nutrition Information per Serving
(1 Square)

Calories: 80

Carbohydrate: 12 grams

Fat: 3 grams

Exchanges:
1 Fruit + ½ Fat

A cornflake topping adds crunchiness to these moist apple treats. They are great in the morning, especially if you're on the run.

Makes 50 Bars

Applesauce Crunch Bars

½ cup (1 stick) unsalted butter, softened

1 cup fructose

1 cup unsweetened applesauce

1 teaspoon vanilla extract

2 cups unbleached all-purpose flour

1 teaspoon baking soda

1 teaspoon ground cinnamon

1 teaspoon ground nutmeg

¼ teaspoon ground cloves

½ teaspoon salt

1 cup dark raisins

Topping

½ cup crushed cornflakes

½ cup chopped walnuts

¼ cup fructose

2 tablespoons unsalted butter, melted

Preheat the oven to 350°F. Lightly butter a 15 × 10-inch jelly-roll pan or spray with no-stick cooking spray.

In a large bowl, using an electric mixer at high speed, cream the butter and fructose for 1 minute or until fluffy. Beat in the applesauce and vanilla. Combine the flour, baking soda, cinnamon, nutmeg, cloves, and salt, and beat into the applesauce mixture. Stir in the raisins. Spread the batter evenly in the prepared pan.

In a small bowl, combine the cornflakes, walnuts, fructose, and melted butter. Sprinkle over the batter.

Bake for 20 minutes or until golden and tester comes out clean when inserted in the middle. Cool in the pan on a wire rack. Cut into 3 × 1-inch bars.

Store: Up to 3 days covered at room temperature.

Nutrition Information per Serving
(1 Bar)

Calories: 75

Carbohydrate: 13 grams

Fat: 2 grams

Exchanges:
1 Fruit + ½ Fat

Aunt Helen's Mandelbrot

My Aunt Helen serves these at almost every family gathering. She makes them with honey and my husband, Richard, now calls her "Honeycake." I sweeten them with fructose. Low in fat, these cookies are light and crunchy. You can make them in advance and freeze until ready to serve.

Makes 36 Cookies

1¼ cups unbleached all-purpose flour

1 teaspoon baking powder

¼ teaspoon salt

4 large eggs

1 cup fructose

3 tablespoons corn, soybean, or safflower oil

1 teaspoon vanilla extract

1 cup blanched almonds, coarsely chopped

1 tablespoon ground cinnamon

Preheat the oven to 350°F. Grease two 9 × 5-inch loaf pans with butter or spray with no-stick cooking spray.

Sift together the flour, baking powder, and salt into a small bowl.

In a large bowl, using an electric mixer at medium speed, beat the eggs for 1 minute. Gradually beat in the fructose, and beat until thick and lemon-colored. Beat in the oil and vanilla. Gradually beat in the flour mixture, mixing well. Stir in the almonds.

Spread a little batter over the bottom of each loaf pan. Sprinkle with a little cinnamon. Repeat until all the batter and cinnamon are used up, ending with batter. You can also just stir the cinnamon into the dough.

Bake for 30 to 35 minutes, or until a cake tester comes out clean. Cool completely in the pans on a wire rack.

Preheat the oven to 400°F.

Invert onto a cutting board and cut into ½-inch slices. Arrange the slices on ungreased cookie sheets and bake for 3 to 5 minutes, or until lightly browned. (Watch carefully—do not burn.)

Store: Up to 1 week in an airtight container at room temperature or up to 3 months well wrapped and frozen.

Nutrition Information per Serving
(1 Cookie)

Calories: 60

Carbohydrates: 9 grams

Fat: 2 grams

Exchanges:
½ Fruit + ½ Fat

Pineapple **P**ecan **B**ars

These easy-to-make bars are special little "good for you" treats, nice to have on hand. They're sure to please all.

Makes 16 Bars

Nutrition Information per Serving
(1 Bar)

Calories: 80

Carbohydrate: 12 grams

Fat: 3 grams

Exchanges:
1 Fruit + ½ Fat

2 large eggs

One 8-ounce can frozen unsweetened pineapple juice concentrate, thawed

¼ cup unsalted butter, melted and cooled

1 teaspoon vanilla extract

1⅓ cups unbleached all-purpose flour

1 teaspoon baking soda

¼ teaspoon salt

1 teaspoon ground cinnamon

½ teaspoon ground ginger

⅛ teaspoon ground nutmeg

One 8-ounce can unsweetened crushed pineapple, well drained

⅔ cup old-fashioned rolled oats

¾ cup coarsely chopped pecans

½ cup golden raisins

Preheat the oven to 350°F. Lightly butter a 12 × 8-inch baking pan or spray with no-stick cooking spray.

In a large bowl, using an electric mixer, beat together the eggs, pineapple concentrate, melted butter, and vanilla. In a small bowl, mix together the flour, baking soda, salt, and spices and add gradually to the pineapple batter, mixing well. Stir in the pineapple, then stir in the oats, pecans, and raisins. Spread the batter evenly in the prepared pan.

Bake for 20 minutes, or until set and lightly browned around edges. Cool in the pan on a wire rack. Cut into 3 × 2-inch bars.

Store: Up to 3 days covered at room temperature.

Ginger Spice Triangles

¾ cup fructose

¼ cup unsulphured molasses

1 cup (2 sticks) unsalted butter, softened

1 large egg, separated

1 teaspoon vanilla extract

2 cups unbleached all-purpose flour

¼ teaspoon salt

1½ teaspoons ground ginger

½ teaspoon ground cinnamon

1 cup chopped walnuts

Preheat the oven to 275°F.

In a large bowl combine the fructose, molasses, butter, egg yolk, and vanilla, and beat until smooth. Combine the flour, salt, ginger, and cinnamon and stir into the batter. Spread the batter evenly in an ungreased 15½ × 10½-inch jelly-roll pan. Beat the egg white and brush it on the top of the dough. Sprinkle the walnuts over the top and press them lightly into the batter.

Bake for 1 hour. Cut into 2½-inch squares while still warm, then cut each square diagonally in half. Let cool in the pan on a wire rack.

Store: Up to 3 days covered at room temperature.

These delicious cookies melt in your mouth. For a different taste, substitute cardamom for the ginger.

Makes 48 Triangles

Nutrition Information per Serving
(1 Triangle)

Calories: 80

Carbohydrate: 12 grams

Fat: 3 grams

Exchanges:
1 Fruit + ½ Fat

Apricot Walnut Squares

The whole wheat flour, wheat germ, and oat bran in these squares add fiber to your diet. The apricots add iron—and wonderful flavor.

Makes 25 Squares

Crust

2 tablespoons unsalted butter, softened

1 tablespoon fructose

1 tablespoon frozen unsweetened apple juice concentrate, thawed

½ teaspoon vanilla extract

½ cup whole wheat flour

2 tablespoons wheat germ

2 tablespoons oat bran

2 tablespoons corn or soybean oil

Filling

½ cup dried apricots, soaked in ½ cup boiling water for 1 hour (Do not discard water.)

2 tablespoons frozen unsweetened apple juice concentrate, thawed

½ cup chopped walnuts

Preheat the oven to 325°F. Lightly butter an 8-inch square baking pan or spray with no-stick cooking spray.

To make the crust, in a medium bowl, using an electric mixer at medium speed, beat the butter, fructose, apple juice concentrate, and vanilla until blended. On low speed, gradually beat in the flour, wheat germ, bran, and oil, and beat until blended.

Press ¾ cup of the crust mixture evenly into the prepared pan. Bake for 15 minutes, or until the edges are lightly browned. Cool in the pan on a wire rack.

Meanwhile, in a small saucepan, combine the apricots, with their soaking water, and the apple juice concentrate. Simmer over low heat for 10 minutes or until the apricots are very soft. Transfer to a blender or a food processor fitted with the metal blade and puree until smooth. Add the chopped nuts and pulse just to mix.

Spread the apricot filling over the partially baked crust. Crumble the remaining crust mixture over the filling and bake for 10 to 15 minutes or until golden brown on top. Cool in the pan on a wire rack. Cut into 25 squares.

Store: Up to 3 days covered at room temperature.

Nutrition Information per Serving
(1 Square)

Calories: 60

Carbohydrate: 9 grams

Fat: 2 grams

Exchanges:
½ Bread + ½ Fat

Almond Peach Bars

These golden bars have a rich peach and almond flavor. For an extra-special treat, serve with a scoop of vanilla low-fat frozen yogurt or a dollop of whipped cream.

Makes 48 Bars

Crust

1 cup unbleached all-purpose flour

⅛ teaspoon salt

½ cup (1 stick) cold unsalted butter, cut into small pieces

2 tablespoons frozen unsweetened apple juice concentrate, thawed

1 teaspoon almond extract

Topping

One 16-ounce can unsweetened sliced peaches, well drained

2 large eggs

½ cup fruit juice–sweetened peach preserves, such as Sorrell Ridge

2 tablespoons warm water

1 tablespoon unsalted butter, melted

¼ cup unblanched sliced almonds

¼ teaspoon ground cinnamon

Preheat the oven to 350°F.

To make the crust, combine the flour and salt in a medium bowl. Using a pastry blender or 2 knives, cut in the butter until the mixture resembles coarse crumbs. Stir in the apple juice concentrate and almond extract and mix well. Press the dough evenly into the bottom of an ungreased 8-inch square baking pan. Bake for 15 minutes or until golden, then cool slightly in the pan on a wire rack.

Arrange the peaches evenly over the partially baked crust. In a small bowl, beat the eggs until foamy. Beat in the peach preserves and water until well blended. Pour the mixture evenly over the peaches. Combine the melted butter, almonds, and cinnamon, and sprinkle evenly over the preserve mixture.

Bake for 20 to 25 minutes, and until the almonds are golden and the topping is set. Cool in the pan on a wire rack. Cut into $1\frac{1}{4} \times 1$-inch bars, and serve at room temperature or chilled.

Store: Up to 4 days covered and refrigerated.

Nutrition Information per Serving
(1 Bar)

Calories: 80

Carbohydrate: 12 grams

Fat: 2 grams

Exchanges:
1 Fruit + ½ Fat

Drop Cookies

Drop cookies are formed by dropping the dough from the tip of a spoon, using a fingertip or another spoon to push the dough onto the baking sheet.

Muesli Pecan Cookies

1 cup unbleached all-purpose flour *or* ½ cup unbleached all-purpose flour
   and ½ cup whole wheat flour
1 teaspoon baking soda
2 teaspoons ground cinnamon
1 cup (2 sticks) unsalted butter, softened
½ cup fructose
2 teaspoons vanilla extract
1½ cups muesli
¼ cup shredded unsweetened coconut (optional)
½ cup dark raisins
½ cup chopped pecans

Preheat the oven to 350°F. Lightly butter 2 cookie sheets or spray with no-stick cooking spray.

Sift together the flour, baking soda, and cinnamon into a medium bowl.

In a large bowl, using an electric mixer, cream the butter and fructose until light and fluffy. Beat in the vanilla. Gradually beat in the dry ingredients, mixing until smooth. Stir in the muesli, coconut, raisins, and pecans.

Drop the dough by teaspoonfuls 1½ inches apart onto the prepared cookie sheets. Flatten slightly with a fork or the bottom of a floured glass.

Bake for 8 to 10 minutes, or until lightly golden. Using a spatula, transfer to wire racks to cool.

Store: Up to 3 days in an airtight container at room temperature, with a fresh apple wedge or piece of bread in the container, or up to 1 month well wrapped and frozen.

Pineapple "Passion" Cookies

1¾ cups unbleached all-purpose flour

½ teaspoon baking soda

½ teaspoon salt

½ cup (1 stick) unsalted butter, softened

½ cup fructose

1 large egg

2 tablespoons frozen unsweetened apple juice concentrate, thawed

¾ cup canned unsweetened crushed pineapple, with its juice

Preheat the oven to 350°F. Lightly butter 2 cookie sheets or spray with no-stick cooking spray.

Sift together the flour, baking soda, and salt into a medium bowl.

In a large bowl, using an electric mixer at high speed, cream the butter and fructose. Beat in the egg. On low speed, beat in the apple juice concentrate and pineapple alternately with the flour mixture until well blended.

Drop the dough by teaspoonfuls, 1 inch apart, onto the prepared cookie sheets. Bake for 10 to 12 minutes, until lightly golden. Using a spatula, transfer to wire racks to cool.

Store: Up to 4 days in an airtight container at room temperature, with a slice of bread in the container.

These luscious cookies do not contain passion fruit—they are consumed with passion! Serve them with sherbet or low-fat vanilla frozen yogurt.

Makes 48 Cookies

Nutrition Information per Serving
(1 Cookie)

Calories: 40

Carbohydrate: 8 grams

Fat: 1 gram

Exchanges:
½ Fruit + ⅕ Fat

Oatmeal Fruit-and-Spice Cookies

No time for breakfast? Packed with fruit and oatmeal, these cookies are perfect for "on the go" with a cold glass of low-fat milk. You can use a single fruit or mixed fruits in these energy-packed treats.

Makes about 24 Cookies

Nutrition Information per Serving
(1 Cookie)

Calories: 60

Carbohydrate: 9 grams

Fat: 2 grams

Exchanges:
½ Bread + ½ Fat

½ cup (1 stick) unsalted butter, softened
½ cup unsweetened white grape juice (not from concentrate)
½ cup fructose
½ cup whole wheat flour
½ cup unbleached all-purpose flour
½ teaspoon baking soda
½ teaspoon salt
1 teaspoon ground cinnamon
¼ teaspoon ground nutmeg
1½ cups old-fashioned rolled oats
1 cup chopped dried fruit

Preheat the oven to 350°F. Lightly butter 2 cookie sheets or spray with no-stick cooking spray.

In a large bowl, using an electric mixer at medium speed, beat the butter, grape juice, and fructose for 1 minute, or until well blended. Combine the flours, baking soda, salt, cinnamon, and nutmeg, and add gradually to the batter, mixing well. Stir in the oats and the dried fruit.

Drop the dough by rounded teaspoonfuls, 1 inch apart onto the prepared cookie sheets. Bake for 10 to 12 minutes, until golden. Using a spatula, transfer to wire racks to cool.

Store: Up to 4 days in an airtight container at room temperature.

Banana Pecan Cookies

1½ cups unbleached all-purpose flour

1 teaspoon salt

1 teaspoon baking soda

½ teaspoon baking powder

¼ teaspoon ground nutmeg

½ teaspoon ground cinnamon

3 large bananas, mashed until smooth

½ cup frozen unsweetened apple juice concentrate, thawed

½ cup corn oil

1 large egg

2 cups old-fashioned oats

½ cup chopped pecans

Preheat the oven to 350°F. Lightly butter 2 cookie sheets or spray with no-stick cooking spray.

In a medium bowl, stir together the flour, salt, baking soda, baking powder, nutmeg, and cinnamon.

In a large bowl, beat the bananas, juice, oil, and egg. Stir in the dry ingredients, and mix well. Stir in the oats and pecans.

Drop the dough by teaspoonfuls onto the prepared cookie sheets. Bake for 10 to 12 minutes until golden. Using a spatula, transfer to wire racks to cool.

Variation: Add 3 tablespoons shredded, unsweetened coconut to the cookie dough.

Store: Up to 3 days in an airtight container at room temperature, with a piece of bread in the container.

A great morning cookie, bursting with the flavor of bananas and pecans. These are also rich in potassium.

Makes 48 Cookies

Nutrition Information per Serving
(1 Cookie)

Calories: 60

Carbohydrate: 8 grams

Fat: 2 grams

Exchanges:
½ Bread + ½ Fat

These light and luscious chocolate peanut butter treats are low-fat and wheat-free.

Makes 36 Cookies

Nutrition Information per Serving
(1 Cookie)

Calories: 20

Carbohydrate: 4 grams

Fat: ½ gram

Exchanges:
¼ Fruit + ⅓ Fat

Cocoa Peanut Butter Meringues

3 large egg whites
¼ cup unsweetened, Dutch-process cocoa
¼ cup fructose
¼ cup unsweetened creamy peanut butter

Preheat the oven to 300°F. Lightly butter 2 cookie sheets or spray with no-stick cooking spray.

In a medium bowl, using an electric mixer, beat the egg whites until stiff peaks form. Beat in the cocoa, fructose, and peanut butter until smooth.

Drop the batter by teaspoonfuls, 1 inch apart, onto the prepared cookie sheets. Bake for 10 to 12 minutes or until dry. Transfer to wire racks to cool.

Store: Up to 4 days in an airtight container at room temperature.

These "healthy" cookies remind me of the Toasted Almond Good

Almond-Carrot Crunch Cookies

1 cup (2 sticks) unsalted butter, softened
½ cup fructose
1 teaspoon almond extract
1 cup unbleached all-purpose flour *or* ½ cup unbleached all-purpose flour and
    ½ cup whole wheat flour

½ teaspoon baking soda

¾ cup Grape-Nuts

½ cup finely grated carrots

¼ cup chopped almonds

Preheat the oven to 350°F. Lightly butter 2 cookie sheets or spray with no-stick cooking spray.

In a large bowl, using an electric mixer, cream the butter, fructose, and almond extract. Gradually beat in the flour and baking soda, mixing well. Stir in the remaining ingredients.

Drop the dough by rounded teaspoons onto the prepared cookie sheets. Bake for 10 to 12 minutes until lightly golden. Using a spatula, transfer to wire racks to cool.

Store: Up to 3 days in an airtight container at room temperature.

Humor Bars my cousin Rozy and I used to buy when the ice cream truck came around. These innocent little goodies are a good way to trick the kids into eating nutritiously. The orange carrot flecks also make them a great cookie for Halloween.

Makes 36 Cookies

Nutrition Information per Serving
(1 Cookie)

Calories: 50

Carbohydrate: 5 grams

Fat: 3 grams

Exchanges:
½ Bread + ½ Fat

These are a
nutritious treat for
Halloween or Thanksgiving.
Pumpkin is a good source
of beta carotene and
vitamin A.

Makes 48 Cookies

Nutrition Information per Serving
(1 Cookie)

Calories: 50

Carbohydrate: 7 grams

Fat: 2 grams

Exchanges:
½ Fruit + ½ Fat

Pumpkin **D**ate **C**ookies

2 cups sifted unbleached all-purpose flour
1 teaspoon baking powder
1 teaspoon baking soda
1 teaspoon ground cinnamon
¼ teaspoon ground nutmeg
¼ teaspoon ground cloves
1 cup (2 sticks) unsalted butter, softened
1 cup fructose
1 large egg
1 cup canned pumpkin puree (unsweetened)
1 teaspoon vanilla extract
1 cup pitted dates, chopped
½ cup walnuts, coarsely chopped

Preheat the oven to 350°F. Lightly butter 2 cookie sheets or spray with no-stick cooking spray.

Sift together the flour, baking powder, baking soda, cinnamon, nutmeg, and cloves into a medium bowl.

In a large bowl, using an electric mixer at high speed, cream the butter and fructose until light and fluffy. On medium speed, beat in the egg, pumpkin, and vanilla. Gradually beat in the dry ingredients, mixing well. Stir in the dates and nuts.

Drop the dough by teaspoonfuls 2 inches apart onto the prepared cookie sheets. Bake for 12 to 15 minutes, until the edges are golden brown. Let cool for 2 to 3 minutes on the cookie sheets, and then, using a spatula, transfer to wire racks to cool.

Store: Up to 4 days in an airtight container at room temperature.

The Frookie Cookie Cookbook

Applesauce Cookies

1⅔ cups unbleached all-purpose flour, sifted

1 teaspoon ground cinnamon

¼ teaspoon ground nutmeg

¼ teaspoon ground cloves

½ teaspoon ground allspice

1 teaspoon baking soda

½ teaspoon salt

½ cup (1 stick) unsalted butter, softened

1 cup fructose

1 large egg

1 cup unsweetened applesauce

⅓ cup raisins

1 cup whole bran cereal

Preheat the oven to 350°F. Lightly butter 2 cookie sheets or spray with no-stick cooking spray.

Sift together the flour, spices, baking soda, and salt into a medium bowl.

In a large bowl, using an electric mixer at medium speed, cream the butter and fructose until light and fluffy. Beat in the egg. On low speed, gradually beat in the flour mixture and applesauce alternately, mixing well after each addition. Stir in the raisins and cereal.

Drop the dough by teaspoonfuls about 1 inch apart onto the prepared cookie sheets. Bake for 12 to 15 minutes, or until golden brown. Using a spatula, transfer to wire racks to cool.

Store: Up to 3 days in an airtight container at room temperature, with a piece of bread in the container.

These spicy cookies are especially rewarding when made in the fall with homemade chunky applesauce.

Makes 48 Cookies

Nutrition Information per Serving
(1 Cookie)

Calories: 40

Carbohydrate: 7 grams

Fat: 1 gram

Exchanges:
½ Fruit + ⅓ Fat

Lemon **D**ate-**N**ut **C**ookies

These delicious cookies are easy to make, travel well, and make a great little gift.

Makes 36 Cookies

Nutrition Information per Serving
(1 Cookie)

Calories: 50

Carbohydrate: 6 grams

Fat: 3 grams

Exchanges:
½ Fruit + ½ Fat

1 cup unbleached all-purpose flour
½ teaspoon baking soda
¼ teaspoon salt
1 cup (2 sticks) unsalted butter, softened
½ cup fructose
2 tablespoons freshly squeezed lemon juice
2 teaspoons grated lemon zest
1 cup chopped pitted dates
1 cup coarsely chopped walnuts

Preheat the oven to 350°F. Lightly butter 2 cookie sheets or spray with no-stick cooking spray.

In a small bowl, mix together the flour, baking soda, and salt.

In a large bowl, using an electric mixer at medium speed, cream the butter and fructose for 1 minute. Beat in the lemon juice and zest. On low speed, gradually beat in the dry ingredients, and beat for 2 minutes. Stir in the dates and walnuts.

Drop the dough by rounded teaspoonfuls, 1 inch apart, onto the prepared cookie sheets. Bake for 10 to 12 minutes until lightly golden. Using a spatula, transfer to wire racks to cool.

Store: Up to 3 days in an airtight container at room temperature.

Coconut Meringues

3 large egg whites

¼ teaspoon cream of tartar

2 tablespoons frozen unsweetened apple juice concentrate, thawed

1 teaspoon almond extract

½ cup shredded unsweetened coconut

Preheat the oven to 325°F. Butter 2 cookie sheets or spray with no-stick cooking spray.

In a medium bowl, using an electric mixer at high speed, beat the egg whites until foamy. Beat in the cream of tartar, and beat until stiff peaks form. On low speed, beat in the apple juice concentrate and almond extract. Gently fold in the coconut.

Drop the batter by teaspoonfuls, 1 inch apart, onto the prepared cookie sheets. Bake for 12 to 15 minutes, until lightly browned. Let cool completely on the cookie sheets.

Variation: Substitute ½ cup ground almonds for the coconut.

Store: Up to 5 days in an airtight container at room temperature.

Light and airy, these easy and delicious meringues are low in calories. They are perfect for Passover celebrations.

Makes 36 Cookies

Nutrition Information per Serving
(1 Cookie)

Calories: 25

Carbohydrate: 3 grams

Fat: 1 gram

Exchanges:
¼ Bread + ⅓ Fat

A hint of almond flavor enhances these quick and easy chocolate cookies.

Makes 36 Cookies

Nutrition Information per Serving
(1 Cookie)

Calories: 50

Carbohydrate: 8 grams

Fat: 2 grams

Exchanges:
½ Fruit + ½ Fat

Chocolate Almond Cookies

½ cup (1 stick) unsalted butter, softened

½ cup fructose

1 large egg yolk

1 teaspoon almond extract

1½ cups unbleached all-purpose flour

¼ cup unsweetened Dutch-process cocoa powder

½ cup unblanched sliced almonds

Preheat the oven to 350°F. Lightly butter 2 cookie sheets or spray with no-stick cooking spray.

In a large bowl, using an electric mixer at high speed, cream the butter and fructose. Beat in the egg yolk and almond extract. Gradually beat in the flour and cocoa, mixing well.

Drop the dough by rounded teaspoonfuls onto the prepared cookie sheets. Using the bottom of a floured glass, flatten the cookies to 2-inch circles. Press the almonds into the cookies. Bake for 8 to 10 minutes until dry. Using a spatula, transfer to 2 wire racks to cool.

Store: Up to 3 days in an airtight container at room temperature.

Orange Nut Cookies

⅔ cup unsalted butter, softened

1 cup fructose

2 large eggs

½ cup freshly squeezed orange juice

1 tablespoon grated orange zest

2¼ cups unbleached all-purpose flour

½ teaspoon salt

½ teaspoon baking soda

½ cup coarsely chopped walnuts

Fruit Juice Icing (page 90), made with orange juice

Preheat the oven to 350°F. Lightly butter 2 cookie sheets or spray with no-stick cooking spray.

In a large bowl, using an electric mixer at high speed, cream the butter and fructose until light and fluffy. Beat in the eggs, orange juice, and zest. In a medium bowl, mix together the flour, salt, and baking soda, and add gradually to the batter, mixing well. Stir in the nuts.

Drop generous teaspoonfuls of dough, 2 inches apart, on the prepared cookie sheets. Bake for about 10 minutes, until golden brown. Using a spatula, transfer to wire racks to cool.

Frost the cooled cookies with the icing.

Store: Up to 3 days in an airtight container at room temperature.

These large cakey cookies are bursting with the flavor of fresh oranges. Serve them with sherbet or low-fat frozen yogurt for a refreshing dessert.

Makes about 36 Cookies

Nutrition Information per Serving
(1 Cookie)

Calories: 70

Carbohydrate: 12 grams

Fat: 2 grams

Exchanges:
1 Fruit + ½ Fat

Lemon Walnut Cookies

These delicious cookies are great anytime. Serve with low-fat sherbet or with sorbet for a refreshing dessert.

Makes 60 Cookies

Nutrition Information per Serving
(1 Cookie)

Calories: 50

Carbohydrate: 8 grams

Fat: 2 grams

Exchanges:
½ Fruit + ½ Fat

1½ cups unbleached all-purpose flour, sifted
½ teaspoon baking powder
¼ teaspoon salt
Pinch of ground ginger
½ cup (1 stick) unsalted butter, softened
1 cup fructose
1 large egg
2 large egg yolks
3 tablespoons freshly squeezed lemon juice
Finely grated zest of 1 large lemon
½ cup walnuts, broken into medium pieces

Preheat the oven to 350°F. Lightly butter 2 cookie sheets or spray with no-stick cooking spray.

Sift the flour, baking powder, salt, and ginger into a medium bowl.

In a large bowl, using an electric mixer at high speed, cream the butter and fructose until fluffy. Beat in the egg and egg yolks. Gradually beat in the dry ingredients, mixing well. Beat in the lemon juice and zest. Stir in the nuts.

Drop the dough by teaspoonfuls 2 inches apart onto the prepared cookie sheets. Bake for 10 to 12 minutes, until golden. Using a spatula, transfer to wire racks to cool.

Store: Up to 4 days in an airtight container at room temperature.

Middle Eastern Oatmeal Sesame Crisps

1 cup frozen unsweetened apple juice concentrate, thawed

½ cup corn or soybean oil

1 large egg, beaten

1¾ cups whole wheat flour

2 teaspoons ground cinnamon

¼ teaspoon salt

1¼ cups old-fashioned rolled oats

½ cup sesame seeds

½ cup chopped raisins

Preheat the oven to 375°F. Lightly butter 2 cookie sheets or spray with no-stick cooking spray.

In a large bowl, stir together the juice concentrate, oil, and egg until well blended. In a small bowl, mix together the flour, cinnamon, and salt and stir into batter, then stir in the remaining ingredients, and mix well. The dough will be stiff.

Drop the dough by teaspoonfuls, 1 inch apart, onto the prepared cookie sheets. Using the bottom of a glass dipped in cold water, flatten the cookies to about ⅛ inch thick. Bake for 8 to 10 minutes, until golden. Using a spatula, transfer to wire racks to cool.

Store: Up to 3 days in an airtight container at room temperature, with a piece of bread in the container.

Sesame seeds impart a delicious crisp and nutty flavor that typifies Middle Eastern desserts. These cookies are a good source of protein, B vitamins, and fiber.

Makes 48 Cookies

Nutrition Information per Serving
(1 Cookie)

Calories: 60

Carbohydrate: 8 grams

Fat: 2 grams

Exchanges:
½ Bread + ½ Fat

A luscious creamy frosting enhances the natural sweetness of the dates, making this a truly special cookie.

Makes 36 Cookies

Date-Nut Cream Cheese Cookies

1 cup finely chopped pitted dates

½ cup frozen unsweetened apple juice concentrate, thawed

1½ cups unbleached all-purpose flour

½ teaspoon salt

½ teaspoon baking powder

¼ teaspoon baking soda

1 large egg

½ cup (1 stick) unsalted butter, softened

¼ cup milk

½ cup chopped nuts

2 ounces cream cheese, softened

1 teaspoon vanilla extract

1 to 2 tablespoons milk (optional)

Preheat the oven to 350°F. Lightly butter 2 cookie sheets or spray with no-stick cooking spray.

In a small saucepan, combine the dates and apple juice concentrate and bring to a boil. Reduce the heat to low, and simmer for 5 minutes. Let cool to room temperature.

Set aside 2 tablespoons of the date mixture for the frosting.

In a small bowl, stir together the flour, salt, baking powder, and baking soda.

In a large bowl, using an electric mixer at medium speed, beat together the egg, butter, and milk for 1 minute. Beat in the remaining date mixture, mixing well. On low speed, beat in the dry ingredients, and beat for 2 minutes. Stir in the nuts.

Drop the dough by rounded teaspoonfuls onto the prepared cookie sheets. Bake for 10 to 12 minutes, until edges are lightly browned. Using a spatula, transfer to wire racks to cool.

To make the frosting, in a small bowl, beat together the reserved date mixture, the cream cheese, and vanilla. If necessary, beat in 1 to 2 tablespoons of milk to make spreadable. Frost the cooled cookies.

Store: Up to 3 days covered and refrigerated.

Nutrition Information per Serving
(1 Cookie)

Calories: 75

Carbohydrate: 12 grams

Fat: 3 grams

Exchanges:
1 Fruit + ½ Fat

A delicious medley of bananas, strawberries, nuts, and coconut makes a naturally sweet fruity cookie. Enjoy them anytime with a glass of low-fat milk.

Makes about 24 Cookies

Nutrition Information per Serving
(1 Cookie)

Calories: 50

Carbohydrate: 7 grams

Fat: 2 grams

Exchanges:
½ Fruit + ½ Fat

Banana-**S**trawberry **N**ut **C**runchies

2 medium bananas, mashed

⅓ cup unsalted butter, melted

1 large egg

¼ cup fruit juice–sweetened strawberry preserves, such as Sorrell Ridge

1 teaspoon vanilla extract

1¼ cups unbleached all-purpose flour

½ teaspoon baking powder

½ teaspoon salt

⅓ cup shredded unsweetened coconut

1 cup coarsely chopped walnuts or pecans

Preheat the oven to 375°F. Lightly butter 2 cookie sheets or spray with no-stick cooking spray.

Combine the bananas, butter, egg, strawberry preserves, and vanilla in a large bowl. In a small bowl, combine the flour, baking powder, and salt and gradually add to the batter, mixing well. Stir in the coconut and nuts.

Drop the dough by rounded teaspoonfuls onto the prepared cookie sheets. Bake for 10 to 12 minutes, until lightly golden. Using a spatula, transfer to wire racks to cool.

Store: Up to 3 days in an airtight container at room temperature.

The Frookie Cookie Cookbook

Refrigerator Cookies

Refrigerator cookie
doughs are shaped
into cylinders or balls
and refrigerated for a few
hours, until firm enough to
cut into thin slices or roll
out and cut into
pretty shapes.

These cookies have
a tendency to spread
and should be placed well
apart on the baking sheets.
The dough can be kept in the
refrigerator for a few days
or frozen for up to
three months.

These cookies are light and have a wonderful peanut buttery flavor. You better hide them from the kids if you want some for yourself: They won't last long!

Makes 36 Cookies

Nutrition Information per Serving
(1 Cookie)

Calories: 50

Carbohydrate: 6 grams

Fat: 2 grams

Exchanges:
½ Fruit + ½ Fat

Irresistible
Peanut Butter Cookies

1½ cups unbleached all-purpose flour
¾ teaspoon baking soda
½ teaspoon baking powder
¼ teaspoon salt
½ cup (1 stick) unsalted butter, softened
½ cup creamy peanut butter
1 large egg, at room temperature
¼ cup frozen unsweetened apple juice concentrate, thawed

Lightly butter 2 cookie sheets or spray with no-stick cooking spray.

Sift together the flour, baking soda, baking powder, and salt into a medium bowl.

In a large bowl, using an electric mixer, cream the butter and peanut butter until light and fluffy. Beat in the egg. Beat in the juice concentrate. Beat in the dry ingredients, mixing well. Cover the bowl with plastic wrap and re-frigerate for 30 minutes.

Preheat the oven to 350°F.

Pinch off generous tablespoons of dough and roll the dough into 1-inch balls. Place 2 inches apart on the prepared cookie sheets. Use a fork dipped in flour to flatten the cookies "crisscross style." Bake for 8 to 10 minutes, until lightly golden. Using a spatula, transfer to wire racks to cool.

Store: Up to 4 days in an airtight container at room temperature.

Almond Butter Crescents

½ cup (1 stick) unsalted butter, melted

¼ cup frozen unsweetened apple juice concentrate, thawed

2 teaspoons almond extract

1 teaspoon vanilla extract

2 tablespoons milk

1½ cups unbleached all-purpose flour

1 cup blanched almonds, finely ground

In a large bowl, stir together the melted butter, juice concentrate, almond and vanilla extracts, and milk until well blended. Gradually add the flour, mixing well. Stir in the almonds. Form the dough into a ball, place on a floured board, and knead for 1 minute to combine the ingredients thoroughly. Do not overwork the dough, or it will toughen. Form the dough into a ball, wrap in plastic wrap, and refrigerate for 1 hour.

Preheat the oven to 325°F.

Pinch off rounded teaspoonfuls of dough and roll into 1-inch ovals. Shape the ovals into 1½-inch-long crescents, placing them 1½ inches apart on ungreased cookie sheets. Bake for 8 to 10 minutes, or until golden. Using a spatula, transfer to wire racks to cool.

Store: Up to 1 week in an airtight container at room temperature or up to 3 months well wrapped and frozen.

These delicate, rich-tasting gems travel well and always make a welcome house gift.

Makes 60 Cookies

Nutrition Information per Serving
(1 Cookie)

Calories: 50

Carbohydrate: 6 grams

Fat: 2 grams

Exchanges:
½ Bread + ½ Fat

High Tea Butterfingers

These cookies melt in your mouth. You can make the dough ahead of time and freeze until ready to bake.

Makes 48 Cookies

Nutrition Information per Serving
(1 Cookie)

Calories: 50

Carbohydrate: 8 grams

Fat: 2 grams

Exchanges:
½ Fruit + ½ Fat

3 tablespoons unsalted butter, softened

3 tablespoons cream cheese, softened

1 teaspoon almond extract

3 tablespoons fructose

1 cup whole wheat pastry flour or ½ cup unbleached all-purpose flour and ½ cup whole wheat flour

¼ cup wheat germ

1 large egg white, slightly beaten

¾ cup finely chopped toasted almonds

In a large bowl, using an electric mixer at medium speed, beat together the butter, cream cheese, almond extract, and fructose for 2 minutes, or until smooth and creamy. Beat in the flour and wheat germ, mixing thoroughly.

Divide the dough in half. Wrap each piece in waxed paper or plastic wrap, and refrigerate until well chilled, about 2 hours.

Preheat the oven to 325°F. Lightly butter 2 cookie sheets or spray with no-stick cooking spray.

Working with one half of the dough at a time, cut off teaspoon-size pieces of the chilled dough and roll between your hands into "fingers" about 2¼ inches long and ¼ inch thick. Dip each cookie in the beaten egg white and then in the chopped almonds, and place them 1½ inches apart on the prepared cookie sheets. Bake for 12 to 15 minutes, or until lightly golden. Using a spatula, transfer to wire racks to cool.

Store: Up to 1 week in an airtight container at room temperature or up to 3 months well wrapped and frozen.

Date-Nut Cookie Tartlets

Pastry

½ cup (1 stick) unsalted butter, softened

One 3-ounce package cream cheese, softened

1¼ cups unbleached all-purpose flour

Filling

1 tablespoon unsalted butter

2 tablespoons frozen unsweetened apple juice concentrate, thawed

1 cup chopped walnuts or pecans

¼ cup chopped pitted dates

1 teaspoon vanilla or almond extract

2 large eggs, slightly beaten

To make the pastry, in a large bowl, using an electric mixer at low speed, beat the butter, cream cheese, and flour together to form a soft dough. Shape the dough into a ball, return to the bowl, and cover with plastic wrap. Refrigerate for at least 1 hour.

Preheat the oven to 350°F.

Divide the dough into 24 pieces, and shape each one into a ball. Press each ball into an individual 1½-inch tartlet mold to form a pastry shell. Set aside.

To make the filling, in a medium saucepan, melt the butter over low heat. Remove from the heat, and stir in the apple juice concentrate, nuts, dates, and vanilla or almond extract. Stir in the beaten eggs, mixing well. Spoon the date mixture into the tart shells, and place on cookie sheets. Bake for 20 to 25 minutes, until lightly browned and puffy on top. Transfer the tartlet molds to wire racks, and let cool to room temperature before unmolding.

Store: Up to 4 days covered at room temperature.

These luscious little tartlets make charming holiday treats. You will need two dozen little tartlet molds for this recipe.

Makes 24 Cookies

Nutrition Information per Serving
(1 Cookie)

Calories: 60

Carbohydrate: 9 grams

Fat: 2 grams

Exchanges:
½ Bread + ½ Fat

Apricot Raspberry Turnovers

½ cup cottage cheese

½ cup (1 stick) unsalted butter, softened

1 cup unbleached all-purpose flour

½ cup fruit juice—sweetened raspberry preserves, such as Sorrell Ridge

½ cup fruit juice—sweetened apricot preserves, such as Sorrell Ridge

In a large bowl, using an electric mixer at medium speed, beat the cottage cheese and butter until smooth. Gradually beat in the flour, and beat for 1 minute, until well incorporated. Knead the dough in the bowl until smooth. Divide the dough in half, and shape each half into a ball. Cover with plastic wrap and refrigerate at least 8 hours or overnight.

Preheat the oven to 425°F. Lightly butter 2 cookie sheets or spray with no-stick cooking spray.

Cut each ball of dough into 8 pieces and form into small balls. On a floured board, using a floured rolling pin, roll each ball into a 4-inch circle. Place ½ tablespoon each of the apricot and raspberry preserves in the center of each circle. Moisten the edges of the dough with water, fold the pastry over the preserves to form a half-moon, and seal the edges together. Crimp the edges using the tines of a fork. Place on the prepared cookie sheets. Bake 10 to 12 minutes, or until lightly golden. Place cookie sheets on racks, let cool slightly. Serve warm.

Store: Up to 3 days covered at room temperature.

These rich and flaky turnovers are delicious and simple to make, but the dough must be made ahead. I like the combination of apricot and raspberry preserves, but feel free to flavor them with your own favorites.

Makes 16 Turnovers

Nutrition Information per Serving
(1 Turnover)

Calories: 50

Carbohydrate: 7 grams

Fat: 2 grams

Exchanges:
½ Fruit + ½ Fat

Chocolate Walnut Cookies

½ cup (1 stick) butter, softened

1 cup fructose

1 large egg

1½ teaspoons vanilla extract

1½ cups unbleached all-purpose flour

½ cup unsweetened Dutch-process cocoa

¼ teaspoon baking powder

¼ teaspoon baking soda

¼ teaspoon salt

½ cup chopped walnuts

In a large bowl, using an electric mixer at medium speed, cream the butter and fructose. Beat in the egg and vanilla and beat until light and fluffy. Combine the flour, cocoa, baking powder, baking soda and salt, and, on low speed, gradually beat into the batter, mixing well. Stir in the nuts. Cover and refrigerate for 1 hour.

Preheat the oven to 350°F. Lightly butter 2 cookie sheets or spray with no-stick cooking spray.

Shape the dough into 1-inch balls, and place 2 inches apart on the prepared cookie sheets. Bake for 8 to 10 minutes, until tops of cookies feel dry. Using a spatula, transfer to wire racks to cool.

Store: Up to 3 days in an airtight container at room temperature.

Chocoholics will add these to their list of favorite cookies. It's difficult to eat just one.

Makes 36 Cookies

Nutrition Information per Serving
(1 Cookie)

Calories: 60

Carbohydrate: 8 grams

Fat: 2 grams

Exchanges:
½ Bread + ½ Fat

Ginger and molasses add a pleasing touch of spice. For a colorful presentation, fill the cookies with a variety of different jams.

Makes 60 Cookies

Nutrition Information per Serving
(1 Cookie)

Calories: 50

Carbohydrate: 8 grams

Fat: 2 grams

Exchanges:
½ Fruit + ½ Fat

Raspberry **G**inger **C**ookies

1 cup (2 sticks) unsalted butter, softened
½ cup fructose
2 tablespoons molasses
2 cups unbleached all-purpose flour
½ teaspoon baking soda
1¼ teaspoons ground ginger
⅓ cup fruit juice–sweetened raspberry jam, such as Sorrell Ridge

In a large bowl, using an electric mixer at medium speed, cream the butter and fructose. Beat in the molasses. In a small bowl, combine the flour, baking soda, and ginger. Gradually add to the batter and beat for 1 minute on low speed. Cover and refrigerate for 1 hour.

Preheat the oven to 350°F.

Pull off 1-inch pieces of dough and roll them into balls. Place 1 inch apart on ungreased cookie sheets. With your finger, make a slight indentation in each ball. Fill each one with ¼ teaspoon of the jam. Bake for 15 minutes, until lightly golden. Using a spatula, transfer to wire racks to cool.

Store: Up to 5 days in an airtight container at room temperature.

Mom's "Sugar-Free" Rugelach

Dough

- ½ cup (1 stick) plus 2 tablespoons unsalted butter, softened
- 5 ounces cream cheese, softened
- 1¼ cups unbleached all-purpose flour

Filling

- ½ cup frozen unsweetened apple juice concentrate, thawed
- ½ cup fruit juice–sweetened apricot or peach preserves, such as Sorrell Ridge
- ½ teaspoon ground cinnamon
- 1½ cups ground walnuts
- 1 tablespoon vanilla extract
- ½ cup raisins

Topping

- ¼ cup milk
- 2 tablespoons fructose
- 1 teaspoon ground cinnamon

This is a fruit juice–sweetened version of my mother's age-old recipe, passed down from her mother. The filling uses ground walnuts instead of the more familiar chopped nuts. These will please even those not fond of sweet cookies.

Makes 48 Cookies

To make the dough, in a large bowl, using an electric mixer at medium speed, beat the butter, cream cheese, and flour until well blended. Divide the dough into 4 portions and cover each with plastic wrap. Refrigerate for at least 2 hours.

Preheat the oven to 350°F. Lightly butter 2 cookie sheets or spray with no-stick cooking spray.

To make the filling, combine the apple juice concentrate and preserves in a small saucepan and cook, stirring, over low heat until the preserves have

Continued

melted. Stir in the cinnamon, walnuts, vanilla, and raisins, and cook, stirring, until the mixture begins to pull away from the sides of the pan. Let cool to room temperature.

On a lightly floured board, using a floured rolling pin, roll out one portion of the dough into a 9-inch circle, rotating the dough often to keep it from sticking. Spread a generous ½ cup of the filling evenly over the dough circle, leaving a border around the edges. With a sharp knife, cut the circle into 12 triangles. Starting at the wide end, roll up each triangle. Bend the ends slightly to form a crescent shape, and place the rugelach, points down, about 1½ inches apart on the prepared cookie sheets. Cover and refrigerate for 45 minutes before baking. Repeat with the remaining dough and filling.

Brush the rugelach with the milk. Mix together the fructose and cinnamon, and sprinkle over the rugelach. Bake for 20 to 25 minutes, or until golden. Using a spatula, transfer to wire racks to cool.

Store: Up to 4 days in an airtight container at room temperature or up to 2 months well wrapped and frozen.

Celebration Butter Cookies

2 cups unbleached all-purpose flour

1 teaspoon baking powder

1 teaspoon salt

¾ cup (1½ sticks) unsalted butter, softened

⅔ cup fructose

2 large eggs

2 teaspoons vanilla extract

I developed these cookies especially for celebrations, because they can be "dressed" for any occasion, from a birthday

72

In a small bowl, combine the flour, baking powder, and salt. In a large bowl, using an electric mixer at medium speed, cream the butter and fructose for 1 minute. Beat in the eggs and vanilla. Gradually add the dry ingredients, beating on low speed, and mix well. Cover and refrigerate for 1 hour.

Preheat the oven to 350°F. Lightly butter 2 cookie sheets or spray with no-stick cooking spray.

On a lightly floured surface, roll out half the dough at a time to ⅛ inch thick. Cut into shapes with cookie cutters, and place on the prepared cookie sheets. Bake for 5 to 7 minutes, until lightly golden. Using a spatula, transfer to wire racks to cool.

Store: Up to 3 days in an airtight container at room temperature.

to Christmas. Frost with Fruit Juice Icing (page 90), if you like, or any of the frostings in this book. Give your kids bowls of nuts and chopped dried fruit and hold a cookie-decorating contest. Or simply sprinkle the cookies with fructose before baking.

Makes 24 Cookies

Nutrition Information per Serving
(1 Cookie)

Calories: 60

Carbohydrate: 9 grams

Fat: 3 grams

Exchanges:
½ Bread + ½ Fat

Linzertorte Fingers

Dough

1½ cups unblanched whole almonds

2½ cups unbleached all-purpose flour

1 cup plus 2 teaspoons fructose

⅛ teaspoon salt

1 teaspoon ground allspice

Finely grated zest of 1 large lemon

1¼ cups (2½ sticks) softened unsalted butter, cut into small pieces

3 large egg yolks

Filling

One 10-ounce jar fruit juice—sweetened raspberry jam, such as Sorrell Ridge

1 large egg

2 teaspoons milk

½ cup unblanched sliced almonds

Finely grind the almonds in the bowl of a food processor fitted with the metal blade.

Sift the flour, 1 cup of the fructose, the salt, and allspice into a large bowl. Add the ground almonds and lemon zest, and mix well. Make a well in the center of the flour mixture and add the butter and egg yolks. Stir together to form a soft dough. Knead gently until smooth. Cover with plastic wrap and refrigerate for 30 minutes.

Preheat the oven to 400°F. Lightly butter a 13 × 9-inch baking pan or spray with no-stick cooking spray.

Divide the dough in half. On a well-floured surface, using a floured pin, roll out half the dough to fit the baking pan. Trim the edges if necessary. Place in the pan, and spread the jam over the pastry. Roll out the other half of dough to fit the pan, and place on top of the jam.

In a small bowl, beat together the egg, milk, and the remaining 2 teaspoons of fructose. Brush the top of dough with this egg glaze. Sprinkle with the sliced almonds.

Bake for 10 minutes, then reduce the oven temperature to 350°F, and bake for 35 minutes, or until golden. Cool in the pan. Cut into 30 rectangular fingers.

Store: Up to 3 days covered at room temperature.

Nutrition Information per Serving
(1 Cookie)

Calories: 90

Carbohydrate: 10 grams

Fat: 5 grams

Exchanges:
½ Bread + 1 Fat

Apricot or **R**aspberry **P**inwheels

Always a favorite, these taste as good as they look.

Makes 48 Cookies

½ cup (1 stick) unsalted butter, softened

1 cup fructose

1 large egg

1 teaspoon vanilla extract

2 cups unbleached all-purpose flour

1 teaspoon baking powder

¼ teaspoon salt

½ cup fruit juice–sweetened apricot or raspberry jam, such as Sorrell Ridge

½ cup flaked unsweetened coconut

¼ cup finely chopped walnuts (optional)

In a large bowl, using an electric mixer at medium speed, cream the butter and fructose. Beat in the egg and vanilla until light and fluffy. Combine the flour, baking powder, and salt and beat in gradually until well blended. Cover and refrigerate for at least 3 hours, or overnight.

Let the dough stand at room temperature just until soft enough to roll out easily.

On a lightly floured board, using a floured rolling pin, roll the dough into a 12 × 9-inch rectangle.

In a small bowl, combine the jam, coconut, and walnuts. Spread evenly over the dough to within ½ inch of the edges. Roll up the dough jelly-roll fashion, starting from a long side. Cut the log in half, for ease in handling, wrap, and refrigerate until firm, 2 to 3 hours.

Preheat the oven to 375°F. Lightly butter 2 cookie sheets or spray with no-stick cooking spray.

Cut the dough into ¼-inch slices, and place 2 inches apart on the prepared cookie sheets. Bake for 8 to 10 minutes, or until the edges are golden. Using a spatula, transfer to wire racks to cool.

Store: Up to 1 week in an airtight container at room temperature.

Nutrition Information per Serving
(1 Cookie)

Calories: 60

Carbohydrate: 10 grams

Fat: 2 grams

Exchanges:
½ Bread + ½ Fat

These traditional cookies are made with a rich, delicate dough that is delicious with fruit fillings.

Makes 24 Cookies

Nutrition Information per Serving
(1 Cookie)

Calories: 60

Carbohydrate: 8 grams

Fat: 2 grams

Exchanges:
½ Bread + ½ Fat

Kolacky

Dough

1 cup unbleached all-purpose flour

⅛ teaspoon salt

½ cup (1 stick) unsalted butter, softened

One 3-ounce package cream cheese, softened

1 teaspoon vanilla extract

¼ cup any flavor of fruit juice—sweetened preserves, such as Sorrell Ridge

1 large egg, beaten with 1 teaspoon cold water for egg wash

In a small bowl, combine the flour and salt. In a large bowl, using an electric mixer at high speed, beat the butter and cream cheese until smooth and creamy. Beat in the vanilla. Gradually beat in the flour mixture, mixing until a soft dough is formed. Divide the dough in half, and wrap each half in plastic wrap. Refrigerate for 1 hour, or until firm.

Preheat the oven to 375°F.

On a lightly floured board, using a floured rolling pin, roll out half the dough to ⅛ inch thick. Using a biscuit cutter or an inverted glass, cut the dough into 3-inch rounds. Spoon ½ teaspoon of the fruit preserves into the center of each dough circle. Lightly brush the egg wash over the edges of the dough circles. Bring the edges of each dough circle up over the fruit preserves to form a triangle leaving some filling visible, and pinch the edges together to seal. Place on ungreased cookie sheets, and brush again with the egg wash. Repeat with the remaining dough and fruit preserves.

Bake for 12 minutes, or until the pastry is golden brown. Let cool on the cookie sheets for 1 minute, then transfer to wire racks to cool completely.

Store: Up to 3 days in an airtight container at room temperature.

No-Bake Cookies

No-bake cookies, are a delicious combination of ingredients often consisting of a chocolate base. As the name implies, they are not baked, but require refrigeration for the ingredients to become chewy and firm.

Tropical Fudge Nut Bars

These cookies are beautiful to look at and heavenly to eat. Serve them at parties or anytime you crave a fudgy, crunchy treat.

Makes 32 Bars

Nutrition Information per Serving
(1 Bar)

Calories: 85

Carbohydrate: 14 grams

Fat: 3 grams

Exchanges:
1 Fruit + ½ Fat

2 cups unsweetened tropical fruit and nut mix
4 ounces unsweetened chocolate, coarsely chopped
¼ cup fructose
¼ cup unsalted butter
Grated zest of 2 large oranges

Lightly butter an 8 × 8-inch baking pan or spray with no-stick cooking spray. Line the bottom with parchment or waxed paper.

Pulse the fruit and nut mix in a food processor fitted with the metal blade until coarsely ground.

Combine the chocolate, fructose, and butter in a double boiler over gently simmering water and heat until butter and sugar are melted and fructose is dissolved, stirring frequently. Stir in the chopped fruit and nuts and half the orange zest. Spread the mixture evenly in the prepared pan. Sprinkle the remaining zest over the top, pressing it in lightly. Refrigerate for 2 hours, or until firm.

Run the tip of a knife around the inside edges of the pan to loosen the chocolate mixture. Carefully turn out onto a board and remove the paper. Turn over and cut into thirty-two 2 × 1 inch bars. Serve at room temperature.

Store: Up to 5 days refrigerated in an airtight container.

Chocolate Macadamia-Nut Clusters

¼ cup unsalted butter

2 tablespoons fructose

2 tablespoons water

¼ cup unsweetened Dutch-process cocoa

⅓ cup dark raisins

2 cups corn flakes

¾ cup chopped macadamia nuts

Combine the butter, fructose, water, cocoa, and raisins in a medium saucepan and cook over low heat, stirring, until the butter is melted and the fructose is dissolved. Stir until well blended. Remove from the heat, and stir in the corn flakes and ½ cup of the macadamia nuts. Spoon the mixture into miniature paper baking cups placed on a baking sheet. Sprinkle the remaining ¼ cup macadamia nuts over the tops. Refrigerate for 1 hour, or until firm.

Store: Up to 5 days in an airtight container in a cool place.

Chocolaty, chewy, and nutty, these cookies are easy to make and perfect for special occasions or house gifts. Toasted almonds or hazelnuts can be substituted for the macadamia nuts.

Makes about 36 Cookies

Nutrition Information per Serving
(1 Cookie)

Calories: 60

Carbohydrate: 10 grams

Fat: 2 grams

Exchanges:
½ Bread + ½ Fat

Chocolate Date-Bran Bars

Makes 32 Bars

Nutrition Information per Serving
(1 Bar)

Calories: 80

Carbohydrate: 10 grams

Fat: 3 grams

Exchanges:
1 Fruit + ½ Fat

6 ounces unsweetened chocolate, chopped

2 tablespoons unsalted butter

2 tablespoons fructose

1 tablespoon molasses

⅔ cup mixed dried fruit, chopped

⅓ cup chopped pitted dates

3 cups bran flake cereal

Lightly butter an 8 × 8-inch baking pan or spray with no-stick cooking spray. Line the bottom with parchment or waxed paper.

Combine the chocolate, butter, fructose, and molasses in a double boiler over gently simmering water and heat, stirring, until the chocolate and butter melt and the fructose dissolves. Remove from the heat, and stir in the dried fruit, dates, and cereal. Spread evenly in the prepared pan, smoothing the top with the back of a spoon. Refrigerate for 1 to 2 hours, until firmly set.

Run the tip of a knife around the inside edges of the pan to loosen the chocolate mixture from the pan. Turn out onto a board and remove the paper. Turn over and cut into thirty-two 2 × 1-inch bars. Serve at room temperature.

Store: Up to 1 week refrigerated in an airtight container.

Savory Cookies

Savory cookies are not sweet but are flavored with fresh herbs, garlic, and cheese. They come in a variety of shapes and are perfect for cocktail parties, as hors d'oeuvres, or just for delicious snacking.

A pleasing garlic cookie accented with the flavor of fresh parsley is a welcome invitation to dinner. They are also pretty and satisfyingly crunchy.

Makes about 36 Stix

Nutrition Information per Serving
(1 Stick)

Calories: 40

Carbohydrate: 7 grams

Fat: 1 gram

Exchanges:
½ Fruit + ⅕ Fat

Parsley and Garlic Stix

1½ cups unbleached all-purpose flour
½ teaspoon baking powder
¼ teaspoon salt
⅓ cup unsalted butter, softened
2 medium garlic cloves, finely chopped
2 teaspoons finely grated onion
1 tablespoon finely chopped fresh parsley
3 large egg yolks
2 teaspoons water
1 large egg white, lightly beaten
Coarse salt for sprinkling

Preheat the oven to 400°F. Lightly butter 2 baking sheets or spray with no-stick cooking spray.

Sift the flour, baking powder, and salt into a small bowl. In a large bowl, using an electric mixer at medium speed, cream the butter for 1 minute. Beat in the garlic, onion, parsley, egg yolks, and water. With a wooden spoon stir in the dry ingredients, then mix with your hands to form a soft dough. You can also use an electric mixer on low speed to blend in the dry ingredients. Mix to form a soft dough. Transfer to a floured surface and knead gently until smooth.

Roll out the dough to a rectangle approximately 14 × 10 inches. Trim the edges, and cut in half crosswise. Using a pastry wheel or knife, cut the dough into thin strips about 7 inches long and ¼ inch wide.

Carefully twist each strip several times, and place on the prepared baking sheets. Brush with the beaten egg white, and sprinkle lightly with coarse salt.

The Frookie Cookie Cookbook

Bake for 15 minutes, or until lightly browned. Carefully remove from the baking sheets with a spatula and transfer to wire racks to cool.

Store: Up to 1 week in an airtight container at room temperature.

Blue Cheese and Walnut Wafers

¼ pound blue cheese, at room temperature

½ cup (1 stick) plus 1 tablespoon unsalted butter, softened

1¼ cups unbleached all-purpose flour

⅛ teaspoon salt

⅓ cup chopped walnuts, plus 48 walnut halves (approximately 1 cup)

Combine the cheese, butter, flour, and salt in the bowl of a food processor fitted with the metal blade, and pulse until the mixture forms a ball of dough. Add the chopped nuts and pulse just to mix in.

Divide the dough in half. Put each half on a sheet of plastic wrap, and shape into a log about 1 inch in diameter. Wrap and chill until firm, about 1 hour.

Preheat the oven to 350°F. Lightly butter 2 cookie sheets or spray with no-stick cooking spray.

Cut the logs of dough into ¼-inch slices and place on the prepared cookie sheets. Top each with a walnut half. Bake for 12 to 15 minutes, until golden. Remove the wafers from the cookie sheets with a spatula, and arrange on a serving platter. Serve warm.

Store: Up to 4 days covered and refrigerated. Reheat in a 350°F oven for 5 minutes before serving.

These rich savory tidbits are perfect with cocktails.

Makes 48 Wafers

Nutrition Information per Serving
(1 Wafer)

Calories: 50

Carbohydrate: 6 grams

Fat: 2 grams

Exchanges:
½ Fruit + ½ Fat

Peanut and Cheese Wafers

Crunchy peanuts and tangy Cheddar cheese flavor these delicious cookies. They are also a more nutritious version of store-bought cheese and peanut butter crackers.

Makes 24 Wafers

Nutrition Information per Serving
(1 Wafer)

Calories: 55

Carbohydrate: 7 grams

Fat: 3 grams

Exchanges:
½ Fruit + ½ Fat

½ cup unbleached all-purpose flour

¾ teaspoon baking powder

½ teaspoon baking soda

¼ teaspoon salt

⅓ cup whole wheat flour

2 tablespoons cold unsalted butter, cut into small pieces

2 tablespoons chunky peanut butter

1 cup grated sharp Cheddar cheese

¼ cup chopped peanuts

1 large egg, lightly beaten

1 to 2 tablespoons milk as needed

GPreheat the oven to 375°F. Lightly butter 2 cookie sheets or spray with no-stick cooking spray.

Sift the all-purpose flour, baking powder, baking soda, and salt into a large bowl. Stir in the whole wheat flour. Cut in the butter and peanut butter until the mixture is crumbly. Stir in the cheese and peanuts. Stir in the egg until well blended, adding just enough milk to hold the dough together.

Transfer the dough to a lightly floured surface and gently knead until smooth. Using a floured rolling pin, roll out ¼ inch thick. Cut out 2-inch rounds with a plain or fluted cutter, and place on the prepared cookie sheets. Bake for 10 to 12 minutes, until lightly golden. Using a spatula, transfer to wire racks to cool.

Store: Up to 4 days in an airtight container at room temperature.

Cheddar Cheese Cookies

½ cup (1 stick) unsalted butter, softened

½ cup solid vegetable shortening

4 cups (approximately 1 pound) finely grated Cheddar cheese

2½ cups unbleached all-purpose flour

½ teaspoon salt

½ teaspoon dry mustard

½ cup chopped pecans or walnuts

Preheat the oven to 350°F.

In a large bowl, using an electric mixer at high speed, cream the butter and shortening for 1 minute, or until fluffy. Beat in the cheese. Beat in ½ cup of the flour, the salt, and mustard, mixing well. Beat in the remaining flour 1 cup at a time.

Fill a cookie press or gun with the dough. Press out ½-inch-wide cookies, placing them 1 inch apart on ungreased cookie sheets. Sprinkle with the nuts. Bake for 8 to 10 minutes, until the edges begin to brown. Using a spatula, transfer to wire racks to cool.

Store: Up to 5 days in an airtight container at room temperature.

These bite-size cheesey cookies are perfect just about anytime. If you're planning to serve them at a party, beware—they disappear fast!

Makes about 90 Cookies

Nutrition Information per Serving (1 Cookie)

Calories: 46

Carbohydrate: 7 grams

Fat: 2 grams

Exchanges:
¼ Bread + ½ Fat

Icings and Spreads

Delicious and easy to make.

Makes about 1 Cup

Nutrition Information per Serving
(1 Teaspoon)

Calories: 20

Carbohydrate: 2 grams

Fat: 1 gram

Exchanges:
⅛ Fruit + ⅕ Fat

Fruit **J**uice **I**cing

1 cup unsweetened frozen apple juice or other fruit juice concentrate, thawed

3 tablespoons unbleached all-purpose flour

2 tablespoons unsalted butter, softened

¼ teaspoon ground cinnamon or nutmeg

Combine the juice concentrate and flour in a small saucepan, and cook over medium heat, stirring, for about 5 minutes, until glossy and thick. Let cool completely.

Using an electric mixer, beat the butter in a small bowl until light and fluffy. Gradually beat in the cooled juice mixture. Beat in the cinnamon or nutmeg.

The Frookie Cookie Cookbook

Cream Cheese Icing

4 ounces cream cheese, softened

¼ cup (more if desired), any flavor, fruit juice–sweetened preserves, such as Sorrell Ridge, to taste

In a small bowl, using an electric mixer, beat together the cream cheese and ¼ cup preserves until smooth. For a sweeter frosting, add more preserves to taste.

Frost cookies and bars just before serving. Once frosted, cookies should be refrigerated.

A fruity creamy topping that will dress up any cookie. You can choose any flavor of preserves to complement specific cookies.

Makes ¾ Cup

Nutrition Information per Serving
(1 Teaspoon)

Calories: 16

Carbohydrate: 3 grams

Fat: ½ gram

Exchanges:
⅕ Fruit + ¹⁄₁₀ Fat

A delicious topping for cookies, toast, or crackers.

Makes 1 Cup

Nutrition Information per Serving
(1 Tablespoon)

Calories: 20

Carbohydrate: 5 grams

Fat: 0 grams

Exchanges:
⅓ Fruit

Date Spread

1 cup chopped pitted dates
½ cup water

In a small saucepan, combine the dates and water, cover, and cook over low heat, stirring often, until thick and smooth. Let cool.

Variation: Stir ¼ cup chopped nuts into the cooked dates. The spread can also be mixed with ½ cup (4 ounces) cream cheese or cottage cheese.

Store: Up to 2 weeks covered and refrigerated.

Prune Spread

½ cup frozen unsweetened apple juice concentrate, thawed

1 cup soft pitted prunes

½ teaspoon ground cinnamon

In the bowl of a food processor fitted with the metal blade or in a blender, process the juice concentrate, prunes, and cinnamon until thick and smooth.

Variation: Add ¼ cup chopped nuts.

Store: Up to 2 weeks covered and refrigerated.

A delicious fruit spread that adds both a wonderful flavor and eye appeal to plain cookies.

Makes 1¼ Cups

Nutrition Information per Serving
(1 Tablespoon)

Calories: 30

Carbohydrate: 7 grams

Fat: 0 grams

Exchanges:
½ Fruit

Index